ArsPoetica is an imprint of Pisgah Press, established in 2011 to publish and promote works of quality offering original ideas and insight into the human condition and the world around us.

Copyright © 2016 Donna Lisle Burton

Printed in the United States of America

Published by Pisgah Press, LLC
PO Box 1427, Candler, NC 28715
www.pisgahpress.com

Cover photography by Donna Lisle Burton
Cover design & layout by A. D. Reed

All photographs and art reproduced in this book
are by Donna Lisle Burton

All rights reserved. No part of this publication may be reproduced, stored in a retrieval system, or transmitted, in any form or by any means, electronic, mechanical, photocopying, recording, or otherwise, without the prior written permission of Pisgah Press, except in the case of quotations in critical articles or reviews.

Library of Congress Cataloging-in-Publication Data
Burton, Donna Lisle
Way Past Time for Reflecting

Library of Congress Control Number: 2016957091

ISBN: 978-1942016281
Poetry/General

First Edition
November 2016

Way Past Time for Reflecting

Poems

Donna Lisle Burton

Acknowledgments

These poems are dedicated to dear friends—you know
who you are—and family, without whom I could not have
traveled this long road to here....

Contents

I. In These Mountains

Bartering 5
Chicory 6
It's About Time: Thoughts at 85 7
In These Mountains 8
Queen Anne's Lace 10
Wood Fires 11
Monday Morning in the Mountains 12
Fresh Corn 13
The Order of Things: for Jan who lost her young daughter 14

II. To My First Child

Out of Work Two Years 21
Cassia 22
Proper Behavior of a First-Time Newly Pregnant Woman 24
For My Beloved Daughter's Fortieth Birthday 26
Daughter Moving Back Home 27
To My First Child 28
April 1, 1980 Census 30

III. The Reason

Tim 35
The Reason 36
Both of Them 38
Grace 39
Always Near 40

IV. Lately

Getting Rid of Summer 45
Mothers' Day at the First Metropolitan
    Community Church of Atlanta 46
Graduation at the Retarded School 48
How Not to Fall Apart at Christmas 50
The Only Medicine 52
Communion: for Patty 53
Naming It 54
Going Back to Ohio 56
9-11-01 58
Letter Home 59

V. Those Days

Too Soon 63
Some Grace 64
Moonsong 65
Alzheimer's: Early Stages 66
Alzheimer's: I 68
Alzheimer's: II 69
Alzheimer's: III 70
Alzheimer's: IV 71
Those Days 72
Caretaker's Lament 74
Having Alzheimer's 75

VI. Latest

Ladies (A Found Poem) 79
Walking at the Mall 80
Oh Brother of Mine 82
Gifts for My Baby Sister Who Could Not Make Her Last
   Trip to Collect Them 84
Older Sister 86
My Fourth Dean 87
Poem for the Man Who Videoed the Fire 88
Doing Less: Settling for More 90
This Heart 91
Patty Brought Me Love and Spring This Morning 92

VII. Addendum

Only Grandchild 97
Only Daughter 98
My Hair 99
A Stolen Day 100
A Birthday Gift for Jill 102
Eternally, Stephen P. Jones 104
Lost/Found Love 105

About the author 109

Way Past Time for Reflecting

Poems

In These Mountains

Donna Lisle Burton

Bartering

In the doctor's office today
the nurse said
*What's this about you
getting out a book of poetry?*
I actually giggled and said,
yes, I did.

I'd like to buy one, he said,
How much?

I need to tell you that my nurse
is also my my bread man
who every week brings us
a loaf of that good stuff
baked by his wife
which when opened smells
like all the warm memories
of childhood and mother and
bread baking day.

Twelve dollars I said.

*How about a month's worth
of bread for a book?*

Bread for poetry:
poetry for bread.
Who's getting the bargain here?

A deal, I said, *a deal!*

Chicory

When I saw all the bright blue
flowers along every road side
in July I finally decided I had
to have some of those for my kitchen
table. And so I stopped one late
morning—they were already not so
blue or so many—and cut me a half
dozen and put them in a vase of water.

In an hour they had turned to pink,
in two hours all the flowers had closed up;
by the next day there was not
a tinge of an open blue blossom.
Some creatures just die in captivity;

Enjoy chicory out on a stroll or
from the car window.

It's About Time: Thoughts at 85

I've decided it's time to start paying attention to my body.
I never have given it much of my time or care.
I've fed it well, kept all its vital organs happy and ticking,
and taken it to the doctor regularly, every three months—
but I mean *pay attention*.

I've always favored my head.
I learned, with the alphabet,
that you can do all kinds of interesting things with it:
enjoy, inform, learn and wonder,
and sometimes, even influence others.

I've certainly babied it, with all this training
and that, graduating from here and there
and going back for more education in this and that
—writing, composing, computing, telling—
I've certainly given in to its demands.

But this poor body never could dance, or swim,
or play tennis, basketball or golf.
It has never climbed a mountain like my son's has,
or saved a troubled swimmer as my daughter's did,
or walked two miles in the mornings as my friend's does.

But just today, I realized this head wouldn't even
be here at all, if my body weren't.
So starting today, it's finally going to get *front row*
in my life and even though it's not the best body in the world,
I'm thanking it every day for just still being here.

In These Mountains

How long do you have to be in a place before
you can claim it?
How long, how long?
I can't feel right
to write
about a place I know
so little of.
Time, I'm talking about.

Yet I know, no one
here forty years
could thrill to that view as I do
starting up the gravel road
and the next five acres
appear as I crest the hill
and catch my breath
every time, day after day.
I marvel at goats scattered, red roofed shed,
roads intersecting, hills here, there
laid out as no artist could.
These are mine.

I claim also the chicory by
the road in the spring
bluer than my son's eyes
and so shy you cannot
collect them—they fade and wilt
right away.

The far off mountains also mine
there beyond the horse barn—
out my window—
which will disappear soon,
covered by tulip poplar
leaves and its flowers
in spring.

One nearby morning
the frost lay thick
on the back row of pines
and the sunlight beamed on them
till they looked ghostly lovely there
and I know only I
saw them.

I didn't mean to own
only to know
And you can claim to know
only so much in a short time.

But seeing to the heart of things
makes knowing surer,
sooner, bending time in
nearer to you, holding it there closely:

You know it.

Queen Anne's Lace

Carefully, I dug up some of my
Queen Anne's Lace, in its second year
in my yard and carried it to my new home
in the mountains. It survived—thrived—
and by August every field around us was
white with Queen Anne's Lace.

When questioned I say but mine
is cultivated, different,
imported. Today I looked at it
closely. It is the same as all the rest.
But it is mine in my yard and not in a field full
of common white flowers.

Wood Fires

And now I suppose I smell the same
as the poor children I once taught
who had this sweet acrid
smell on their bodies, hair, clothes
which I could not name as
wood fires were not then in my life.

I thought it had to do with
poor, lack of bathrooms, running
water and infrequent and spotty
bathing. I felt sorry for and
superior to them.

Now when I walk into
the dress shop, does the clerk
know about wood fires
or does she simply turn her back
on me and ask the next lady
May I help you?

Monday Morning in the Mountains

I put the basket of clothes in
the Flexible Flyer, pull it to the side yard.
As if I had no other choices, I hang
the wet clothes up, one after one.
And when I prop them up with my new prop
made by my new husband,
they do what I put them up there for—
dance and blow and shake in the breeze
and I sit in the yellow chair all the while
and also watch the horses in the next yard
clothes flying, horses eating, sky bluing
putting on a show for me this
wash day morning.

Fresh Corn

There is a sign near his driveway
saying FRESH CORN. It looks
like the same words I see in the
grocery store—fresh corn. But

when we drive up to the corn
grower under his hemlock tree for shade
and ask for a dozen ears and he has
only five, and he asks yellow or white
and goes into the field right there
and gets them from the stalk
I tell you friend
that is FRESH CORN.

The Order of Things:
For Jan who lost her young daughter

It is March and whether
we will it or not
Spring is here.
Through the giving soil
green shoots push up
into the sun, the rain.

Even when we don't care
buds will appear on the
wild redbud trees
and willow is yellow
with new life.
Last fall's leaves still cling
to the white oak
but the maple is already
covered with new leaf pink.

Life goes on
Spring comes
air softens
days grow longer:
it is the order of things.

Sometimes in the spring
a killing frost comes
and in an eye-blink
the bud is burned
the blossom dead.
We mourn this loss.
We think nature cruel
uncaring

But sometimes
this is also
the order of things.

Nature knows of this
dispensation
the budding
blossoming
freezing, dying.

But I think it is not
in the order of things
that mothers
bury
their children.
Their pain was in birthing
and tending, training and caring for the tender things.
Watching and worrying over their first day of school,
first loves, first children.
Death is not in
the order of things.

But
it is spring
and whether we willed it or not
the daffodils have yellowed the hillsides
the forsythia too
the trillium
the violets are trying to hide
but you can find them.

Spring is in order.
There is rebirth. Renewal.
Even if we don't care.
Even if somehow we must
go on, thrive, grow, in spite of the
killing frost.

Even if your daughter will
never see Spring again.

And one day, Spring will be
beautiful again
in spite of it all.

This is
the order of things.

To My First Child

Donna Lisle Burton

Out of Work Two Years

How astonishing it is that at 83
I am just beginning to know my
woman child, first born,
gone from me these last thirty years.

All kinds of adjectives fill my mouth:
stubborn, kind, handy, thoughtful, tough,
able, direct, soft, determined, logical
and surely dear.

And I feel damaged by all the
indignities you have unjustly borne
and wonder that you can still walk upright
with the pressures you have and do carry.

You think you've come home in defeat.
You're wrong my forty-nine-year-old.
You've come home to re-group and
to find out at last who you really are,

what kind of precious substances you're
actually made up of,
and how much this person you call mother
unconditionally loves you.

Cassia

Heartache child
all through the years
heartache.

Friends always hard to find
and keep, always
beneath your person.
Never, never sure of
my love (why not?).

Started with having
to be born, lovely perfect child,
a gift of softness, steel, fear,
full of fear.
Anxious, trusting where you shouldn't
and not when you should.
Full of resentment but unable to speak of it.

Adores her child but cannot be firm with him
Stuck with her husband, afraid to let go
of him.
What is her work; she doesn't know.
She can be neat but can live
in ruins for more days than I ever could.

I want to make the world all safe for her
and place her in it.
She can't take charge in her marriage
her mate is too obstinate.

I long to be with her more, give her comfort
not to mention all manner of pretties.
Her skin so soft, hands so small, voice so lovely.

She is gold on silk, pearls on monks-cloth.

My first love,
my beauty,

my heartache.

Proper Behavior of a First-Time Newly Pregnant Woman

It is important from day one
you talk to that little seed;
talk and sing too.
And when you are very tired,
just hum and stroke your
still small belly.

Every day, affirm that
while she had her reasons for
wanting to be born of you,
you know he is only love,
and is coming here to teach you
just that.

Read her funny stories
and sagas too,
that bring tears to your eyes.

While you can,
hold that belly and skip and dance,
for lightness is delighted in
even by tiny seeds.

And one day, when it finally
dawns on you that this
is for real and every day you grow
larger and rounder
and there's no changing your
mind and going back now—
feel
that trapped state
all over.

Then know that
soon
your will have your
body back again—
and a fat soft baby—
all yours—
to hold—
and adore.

For My Beloved Daughter's Fortieth Birthday

I remember your birth so well,
lotus growing out of the mud
of my being. Gift to me,
after so many years in sterile academia.
You became my love,
my heart, my raison d'être.

And I know you understand
for you now have your own
golden-haired one.

How to greet you, how
to celebrate this day and
other birthdays?

Every day I would give you a draught of
peace, even before your morning eyes opened.
I would take away all fears,
real and imagined—and make pearls
of them to string around your neck.
At every hint of impatience I would
whisper in your ear *serenity, serenity.*
For days of darkness I would ask the sun
itself to shine wherever you are.
And when you became overcome with
loneliness I'd ask the world
to come visit you, one by one.

But when you already have the world
in your baby boy, what more is there
to want?

Daughter Moving Back Home

What I want to say about all this is
what else is one to do?
There is a need: not an imagined one or
one with lots of choices attached,
but a need with few or no
best choices.
So you take the only choice
and try to make the best of it—
with a smile yet.

We were all free floating
in pain, needing help
not asking for it
but with that kind of need
there's no asking to do.

So you do what's there to be done
And hope that
because there was no debatable issue
things would just fall into place and
come together as it must.

A few years and a few months later
and we're still speaking to each other.
Must have been something
right about it.

To My First Child

Just because I had you
doesn't make you mine.
Mine to hold, to know—
certainly not to know.
And yet because I had you
I must come to know you,
trying, always failing,
trying but you
holding me off.

As if to say
after all
*you don't own me
know me.*

I knew you then
darling girl,
sweet lotus flower
blue-eyed blonde
perfect round head
but even then you held back.

I still see you fold up
your blanket with tiny fingers
making a little pad to put
in your mouth to suck on,
so as not to insist: *I am hungry;
do something about it!*
I had to come to you,
find you, quiet, sucking
on that blanket,
offer you the breast or bottle
for you did not cry, demand.

And maybe that's it.
Maybe you've been saying
all these years
Find me mother,
find me!
I cannot ask.
I just can not ask.
I simply can't.

April 1, 1980 Census

Do you remember, daughter?
A decade ago today
we were on a bus heading north.
Leaving wisteria behind,
we hit snow in Cincinnati
and arriving at Easter noon
found Columbus covered by it.

Your Papa was glad to see his Alabama girl,
all but six and very able to read.
He looked well, but was red-faced angry
about the old bitch who wouldn't pay
what she'd agreed for his paint job.

We ate Easter ham and candied yams
and you sat on his great lap
telling tales that made his face
red with laughter.

By the next day he was
flat with pain,
groaning with it, angry at it.
In a week he was sliced
across his chest
and did not know me when
I saw him last.
The day before your late April birthday
he was dead.

By June new life was in me.
Your brother, born at next February's end
was not in that census, nor was my father
though it counted him.

Now ten years later, a new census,
a nine-year-old with my father's name
counted
as your Papa will never be
counted again.

The Reason

Donna Lisle Burton

Tim

Child of my too late to have children
years.
Surprise child, boy child,
so different from your sister.

Made up for your sister's
non-demanding—in spades!
No bottle; the breast!
I will walk; now!

And he said *star* at seven months.
Yes he did.

You are the one I had to give
some of our house to
when we left it forever.
Your marks around a kitchen door frame,
now a frame around a picture
of words and hand-prints of you,
and hanging in your first home.

I hope I know you
as well as you, me.
For you don't let this
gray head, saggy body
fool you. You know
that strong yet frail
looking person
inside there is not only
your mom
but her own person.

The Reason

My second and last born,
child of my middle age,

forty-one when you finally got here.

You made one of each, my sensitive serious
blue-eyed boy.
Brighter than me and his father
but sad—always sad.
Achiever, doer,
hope you can find
someone who will love
you for being.
Very different from me
yet he is the one I'm
most like, akin to.
Very bright, a go getter;
he can take his world
and put it in its place.

I will never see his child;
perhaps not even his love.

When he breaks forth
with a smile, teasing,
it is a delight.

He has tried very hard
to make sense of and acceptance of
his dad and now, me.
Deliberate, perfectionist,
yet laid back, lover of
animals and does very
well with little children
accepting and playing with,
putting up with.

He's Auntie's boy.
So like his dad in
liking good food, nice cars,
good clothes, simple
personal wants.
Hard to see another's
point of view if it's subtle.

Loner, expecting
little of anyone, anything.
Handsome, very
vulnerable, a hard
exterior but soft inside.

My blue-eyed boy-man.
Son of my middle years.
Heart child.

A reason for that marriage.

Both of Them

For ten years now
I have known that
my young son would never
tell me of a heart break
fear of the dark
blister on his thumb
for he knew my
already sadness
would make one more pain
too much.

I never knew who he was.

Now today
my grown daughter confesses
she could not tell me of her pain
when pencils would not go right
when word sounds made her spell funny
and I asked why didn't you tell
me then, pony tail, long curls girl.
And she said you were already
always smile-less, inner;
I couldn't make you
more upset.

Of course,
I never knew her
either.

Grace

Again, this year, my only son
is not coming home for Christmas.
"Come and see me next year," he says
and we talk about that—when
would be the best time for each
of us. Thoughts of all Christmases
past do not seep out of my memory
and into my voice.

A *why not* placard flashes up
like the old cash register signs
but pops back down and my voice is
speechless.
I behave like he would want me to—
no guilt-inducing questions or inflections
in my voice that make the words
I say something other than
the words I say.

I put down the phone
and wonder how I did so well.
The cash register key that says *grace*
pops up and I sigh *thanks*
to whatever angels watch over
tired old mothers who always want
only to see their children at
Christmas time.

Always Near

Time was
when I would speak of *when*
you would stop me with
Let's don't talk about this
and I knew you were
still too tender.

Lately you can actually say
When you're no longer here...
but I can still feel the pain
in your words, your voice.

There seems nothing I can say
right now to abate it,
for to you now,
death means only
forever gone.

What you don't know yet
is that after that night
I will be
wherever you are
every day
and that love
can help one
see that.

Lately

Getting Rid of Summer

These first days—when the air
puts my sweater on me,
when, if I think about it I can
make myself shudder with it—
liven my bones.
After the raging summer
whose days enervate me

this sudden trembling is
the psyche's way of shaking off
that crater, stupor
and saying yes I'm sparkling again
just like that breeze tumbles the leaves
this way and that and
shakes off summer.

Mothers' Day at the First Metropolitan Community Church of Atlanta

The spirit was so high today that
the rainbow banner that ran
along one side under the gold cross
across the front of the room
was shaking with it.
And no wonder:
I'd be one glad gay to have
my own church where I am
okay
and no one's telling me how
ashamed God is of me.
I'd get in the choir and sing and clap too
like my friend Trudie, up there,
smiling, her mouth and eyes wide open
swaying and clapping to the music—
and I thought she just went there
because her husband is bisexual.

She's there because she loves it

As does the angel who's the lovely
red headed soloist whose voice is so
beautiful I thought she must be
mouthing it, tape in the background.
To find out, she's as straight as the
Bishop of Canterbury and
on the Braves' at home days she's the
Star Spangled singer

and she's also there because she loves it.

Then there's my friend's mother
next to me, as up and down
as any flag pole who gets more hugs
than anyone because she's
ninety and their newest member

and she loves being there.

I too am straight like my
hair used to be at ten
when Shirley Temple curls
abounded and I was envious.
But I tell you I know it doesn't matter what
I or my friend or her mother are,
we are all brothers and sisters and I
never felt it so much as today when
in the communion circle
there was straight me,
grandma, the bisexual husband,
and the black lesbian lady who
is a car mechanic and we had
communion and hugged and kissed

and I can't remember when I
ever enjoyed church so much as today

on Mothers' Day at the
First Metropolitan Community Church of Atlanta.

Graduation at the Retarded School

At first it looks like any school.
Ivy twirled around the room dividers
fake flowers making the
gym look lovely for once.
Parents dressed to the occasion.
And then the graduates march in to the
traditional Pomp and Circumstances.

But look again
that one with the distorted face
the five look-alike Down's children
and that pretty girl whose photo
would show nothing amiss.
Just like children
some are smiling
some silly
some very sober.
The parents of the pretty one
whisper to her *slow down*
as she goes by them.
The father with his
expensive camera goes up front
to shoot as she's handed her
diploma.

All have met the graduation requirements:
they are at least 21 years old.

Only their parents have the heavy hearts,
knowing their best, their protected years,
are behind. And the rolled up paper
tied with green satin ribbon is
only something to frame and

hang on their walls,
entitling them to
no job, no profession, and
for some one day, heralding
an entrance to a less happy
institution than
public school.

How Not to Fall Apart at Christmas

I was so afraid I would fall apart
last Christmas that
I handled myself more tenderly than
fresh flowers.

I gave myself lots of sleeping-in days,
delicious afternoon naps.
One day I felt self-indulgent and I spent
almost the entire day working on
a summer scene jigsaw puzzle.

I wore warm clothes that were soft
against my drying skin and colors
that made me easier to look at.
And instead of stuffing myself with
homemade sweets, I treated myself
and ate just a few.

I played the winter solstice CDs
before and after
the winter solstice.
One day I turned off the radio
as I heard the Messiah start
and painted a snow scene instead

I thought I was home free by Christmas eve
and then I was caught in a mall with
O Come All Ye blaring at me and
I just couldn't get out until it was nearly
over and found my cheeks wet as
thoughts raced back to all those years
all those years......

I got in the car quickly
and drove away from those
songs, those lights, those trees
back to my house where
I could breathe again
slowly, slowly,
in and out, in and out...
where I could just let
Christmas come and
not fall apart.

The Only Medicine

My friend's laughs are
the greatest.
They're belly laughs
head back and roar laughs
bring tears to the eyes laughs.
And after a while
everything's funny—
the blue sky—
the brown dog over there;
everything's funny.

Except his sadness
which is just as great.

He does not say my son is broken
and I don't know how to fix him
but his voice is weeping
when he speaks his name.

He does not say this pain is with me
every hour and when I awaken in the
night it is my first thought.
But the circles under his eyes
are dark and cut deeply into his face.

He does not say my heart is broken
then you notice it
sticking out of his shirt
at a strange angle.

How to comfort a friend
whose pain is so great
he can do nothing but
laugh?

Communion: For Patty

We had lunch together
and talked of
        chicken with roasted peppers
        children leaving their shoes on stairs
        cottages on Cape Cod
        growing older, using time well
        painting my grandson's picture
        where we might find
                real spiritual direction.

So why is it after we parted
I felt like
        I had eaten a feast
        my feet were without will, dancing
        my home was a lighthouse
        my bones were sweeter, no age at all
        my hands made light whatever they touched
        I'd been to a monastery for a
                week of silent retreat?

Naming It

We've been on a journey, my friend
and what a trip it's been! We've gone
to the moon together
but that was just the beginning:
we've circumnavigated the universe
with no ship
only holding each others' hands.

We've looked into places
where the wise ones
stay out of
but we went, you
usually leading the way,
pulling me along
like a willing but frightened
pup.

What do we call
where we've gone
how we got there,
this journey?

Intimacy, a friend offered.

Yes.

Is that why then
I couldn't find it
in Webster's
because I had no name for it?

We gave it lots of names
all of which were
too short in the front
too long in the back
too tight in the seams
or hanging down around
the ankles.

Intimacy,

Yes.

No wonder then that
when I saw it leaving
I heard these sounds like
a broken winged bird crying,
coming from a nearby throat,
far into the night and early dawn
that eased only when
daylight made
all things clear
and all pain
understandable:

journeys do end.

Going Back to Ohio

When I cross that river there is a
click
and I'm connected again
That part of me that is still here
connects
and there is a wholeness now.

Sometimes, after I'm here a while
I notice the clicking gets
softer
more like a little thum.
And this is because the place
has changed so that
there is little of me still there.

Sometimes there's no clicking at all;
I have no history there:
the new library
the big new technical school.

But in the old neighborhoods
in Steubenville Ohio
it would be like a metal detector
if I could hear the clicking.

Instead it is just me again
at nine on the back porch swing
of a summer night, looking at the
light bulb cross on the church
above the buildings

Or me at fifteen on the same swing
another house and summer night
watching the boys at the corner
talking laughing under the
street light.

I am still there.
This place has my history
and a little of my self
is always there
waiting for that
connection
that clicking
when I return.

9-11-01

The mind cannot conceive
what it knows has happened.
When I think of the terror on those
planes I have to stop.

I can't know that terror.

It is like a dream of falling and
you know it's a dream but you
keep falling, it's desperate
and horrifying but
before you hit bottom
you know you will always
wake up

but not this day.

Letter Home

My dear children,
it is exactly as I
thought it would be:
essential.
Nothing surprising, superfluous
no exotic anything.
I always knew I would be
ready for it: how else could it be?
I am so glad I wasted few moments
pondering on it, trying to decide
what it would be like
when of course, no one
could.
But when it happens you know
immediately that this is as
you always knew it
would be.

And so like everyone else here,
I'm handling it
smoothly, fine.
It fits as being born and living did,
better even somehow
without all the endless
choices, decisions,
and instead only the
quiet and lightness of
a fine mid-May day.

And I'm just fine.

Those Days

Too Soon

There has not been enough time yet,
knowing you, to remember you
when I leave. This takes time and practice.
And there has not yet been enough of either.

So when I leave, although I will have
spent two whole days looking at your
face, at every wrinkle, puffy place—
hair of black for your mustache,
hair of white in your beard and head,
brown eyes that always look a little sad—
until I see you again
I will forget all this.

Because there has not yet been time
to etch all of you into my memory,
my brain, so when I see you again
it will be as always before, a delight
to see that you do indeed have
this face, this body, those eyes, these hands—
that are surprisingly pleasing, strong,
and beautiful—and I will have verified one
more time that I am glad to have met you
and
to be coming to know you
until the etching comes.

Some Grace

In our seventh decade
we have found one another
and peace
such as I have not known.

It is the joy of being
in the same room with you,
hand on my leg that says
I claim her—
saggy breasts, dimpled thighs,
shelf belly and all—
and so I see it has nothing
to do with those things.

It has more to do with
what love is:
an aria, chicory blue petals,
shells that you have to keep
when you find them.

Grace

Moonsong

The moon is low in the sky, and
shining through our bedroom
window, its light on your face,
your white hair, your resplendent
male fabric.

How swell to touch and hold you
your hand on my arse wordlessly saying
I'm glad you're here.

I smile in the darkness
and stroke your beard
lightly
so you do not awaken.

Alzheimer's: Early Stages

Your eyes don't dance as they once did.
They are somewhat tired, lifeless
but still quite beautiful.
You are thinner:
we must get you a new belt;
eight extra inches are unnecessary.

You stoop a little more.
But on the phone your voice,
at least, seems unchanged
and still makes me smile and feel
warm in places
that no longer seem to function
as before.

When driving
you ask, *do I turn here, is this
the right street, is it in this place?*
And I hope I answer
casually
as if you didn't ask the same
yesterday—or an hour ago.
But you can still drive,
gratefully.

You ask
repeatedly
about the date, day, appointments, plans
and love to tell old stories of long ago
flawlessly.
You never speak of those things
you're having to let go of
but seem to give them up
wordlessly.

All these changes of the past year
are small, relatively unimportant.
I just don't think a lot about

Next year.

Alzheimer's: I

It is indeed
Spring again,
even though the pear decided
only leaves this year, not blossoms,
and it is 50 outside
and the crocuses have long been gone.
I know the wren who sat in the
lattice-work yesterday, sending and receiving
wren messages from a far off wren,
will soon have me hunting for her nest—only
to peek—not touch.

My husband put up that lattice-work
three years ago when such a job was
easy for an old carpenter's hands—and
three and four and five years ago when
everything was easy for his hands.

Now he stands and looks at work
he used to do easily
and puzzles; is it
this way or that
a screw here
or there?
What is it I'm trying to build?

But spring is back and although
the pear tree didn't bloom this year
almost
everything else
is just the same.

Alzheimer's: II

Sometimes I just sit and
think about things
like love and justice and luck
and when I'm feeling very smart
I know what they all mean
and could tell you too.

Other days I simply cannot
define *small*; is it like little,
just a bit, a tad, wee,
or simply not big?

My husband says
periodically,
"I'm the luckiest person in the world."
I never say that, not even
on my very best days
when I feel smartest
and most smack sure—
not even those days when I know
what love and justice and luck
are.

Tell me, I ask, how is that so?
"I've got good health, a loving family
and you," he says.

And Alzheimer's, I say to myself.
Isn't he lucky?

Alzheimer's: III

It is the first day of Spring and—
it is okay that I repeat
today's date five times today
for I can judge my patience
quotient by examining if
I said it louder the second time,
frowned the third
and certainly if I say
"I already told you that,"
after the fourth—
and it's so pretty out.

No accolades for patience.
Little enough to offer
when *I'm* not asking for the third time
when *I'm* not forgetting I just asked
for the fourth time
when *I've* not forgotten already
what I asked, so that the answer
makes no sense.

Patience with icing—
that's what that deserves.
Even if it were not
the first day of Spring.

Alzheimer's: IV

And now, a year later,
he can finally say,
as if it is just a fact,
I don't drive anymore;
better safe than sorry.

It took a year for him to say that.
Six months ago Dr. K asked
if he had given up driving
and he said *Oh no, I can drive*
and he hadn't for months,
but his heart hadn't given it up.

Now when I mention my driving
here and there he offers
I could drive, but better, etc., etc.
I agree and praise his wisdom.

His heart has given up too.

Those Days

I knew he had forgotten my birthday,
my age, our wedding anniversary,
and wasn't certain who this woman-child
was, about to take him for the day—
sister, niece, neighbor or just a friend?
Daughter was not even a maybe choice
some days.

After an all-day outing he could not
tell me the places his group
went or name even one of
them or what they ate. A day spent
with a great grand I know he enjoys
but he cannot tell me her name at all
any days.

I was even getting used to seeing
Alzheimer's meant one cannot do
as well as know; batteries go in
only one way. Yet once in a while
he will seem to recall how this worked
and surprise you and do it properly
certain days.

But when he looked into my eyes one night
and said *Tell me, what is your name?*
I know I gasped before I answered him
although I did not let it show
that my heart had broken some that day.
But he still seems to know who I am
most days.

So now and then I test him and I ask
who am I and usually he smiles and
says *You're my love.*
But what is my name?
and he says it. But what freezes
my heart is he won't know it
or who I am at all
one day.

Caretaker's Lament

He looks a lot the same
but not the eyes; they're dull.
The face is not lit up with life—instead
it's sober, maybe even a little frightened.

Where has my husband gone?

I grow weary some days of being in charge
making it all happen
for if I were to put down my baton
the dishes would not get washed
the bed made
the birds fed.

Maybe one day I should just
stop directing
and see for myself,
how I alone am causing
our life to go on
in some kind of fashion.

But would it at all
if I just quit calling all the shots?
I think I'm afraid to try it
for then I'd be faced with it.

I can't get sick
I can't be tired.
I have to be on the ball.
I must stay in charge.

But what if I didn't just one day?
Just One Day

Then what?

Having Alzheimer's

I hate that I get lost in the
every-day-ness of it;
that I'm unusually good at being patient,
don't even blink at answering the same
question five times in five minutes.
I explain things slowly
without even raising my voice;

supervise your showers
as if you were my child instead
of the strong handsome Adonis
I fell so much in love with that
I was giddy and strangely unpredictable
and feeling those stomach butterflies
that haven't been there since seventeen.

And when I think about it,
I miss all that
and them
and you.

And if I'd let myself
I'd keen for want of them,
and being unable to behave always
exactly as I feel;

for I too am lost—
in perfectly acceptable behavior.

Latest

Ladies (A Found Poem)

The other day I was in the waiting room
at the dentist's office.
Across from me
sat one white gal, alone, and next to her,
two younger black gals who knew each other.
This white gal was looking at a magazine
just like everyone else in that room
except the two black gals who were talking
and laughing, now and then, in quiet tones.

When the white gal leaned over to get
something from her purse that sat on the floor,
the July issue of *Ladies Home Journal*
fell off her lap,
and onto the floor.

Immediately

the black lady next to her picked it up
and handed it to her, and
the white gal held out her hand to receive it,
took it,
continued reading it, never ever
once turning her head to look at
the black lady and
never saying a word.

The black ladies looked at each other
and smiled.

The white gal
kept on reading her magazine.

Donna Lisle Burton

Walking at the Mall

Pointedly, people smile at me.
Many actually speak as I make
my rounds.
Doors open as if by magic
and I look to see the eye I tripped
and find instead a fortyish woman.
Discounts are offered without even
inquiring of my eligibility.
The world is gentler, nicer now.

The big secret is
I am not.
I still would not speak first.
I am inward as a monk.
Do not feel special
that I am still alive.
Grateful, lucky are the descriptors.
And in spite of the fact
my walking shirt has Willie's face on the front
and *have a Willie nice day* on the back,
it's my secret fun and I have
no comment about it.

This gray hair is not me.
I know who's inside:
I am a thirtyish auburn haired gal who falls
into dancing around the kitchen
to slow '50s tunes on the radio;
who still believes in the
pit-of-the-stomach feelings

stirred by that handsome man
walking just ahead of me;
who wonders why they think
gray hair and other baggage of old age
make me friendlier, gentler and nicer,
turn me into something
I never was

And still am not.

Oh Brother of Mine

Your intelligence and good looks
were beacons to me in a dark childhood,
even though you too made shadows
in my life
of such magnitude that I still
feel vestiges of them
seventy-five years later.

And strange as it may sound now,
as they memorialize you as a
devoted Christian man,
you, a much younger you,
were my iconoclast
and freed my journey to
learn in very other directions.

I honor you for that this day.
And for being so tender and loving
with me as to often slip, call me
by your daughter's name,
on our every third week
phone calls.

And I will also love you forever
for always wanting to speak to
my husband at each call,
even long after you knew
he no longer knew
who you were.

Peace, my brother.
I am so happy that

at last
it has come
to you
now,
forever.

Donna Lisle Burton

Gifts for My Baby Sister Who Could Not Make Her Last Trip to Collect Them

I shopped Friday, picked
carefully those foods I knew
you would savor.
I made the peach cobbler of course and it
now sits in its juice awaiting
someone to eat it.
The crab and shrimp casserole I
kept a secret, wanting to
surprise you,
you wondering how I had
energy to do all that.

But before the food, the meals,
I wanted to satisfy the pith of you
with my yard that has
never looked lovelier.

First, driving in, with the oval
daylily bed in its most beautiful
year of lilies from buttery-white through cerise
and all yellows, reds, pinks, oranges, in between;
the whole six dozens bloomed this
year because for once the deer
didn't eat them, our dog
keeps them away.
The hosta too blooming as it did when
in our mother's backyard where it once was
when we were both young enough to
walk around in it.

You would have marveled at the rudbeckias in the side
yard, deep orange and the pink coneflowers;
the six-feet-tall sunflowers that decided to grow this year
by the six-foot-tall bird-feeder,
some bird accidentally knocking seed to the ground.
Right now a yellow finch sits atop, hardly
distinguishable from the flowers.

The just barely pink-green-white calla lilies
would be the greatest surprise.
I never spoke of them before
and how their cheap Easter grocery store purchase
has given me such joy the last two years;
or the purple-blue spreading geranium right
off the porch that would be taller than I am
if I were to lie down beside it.

I cry to think of the laughs we would have had
in the evening, drinking wine and eating cheeses
sated everywhere one could be sated
overflowing too with love we
hardly speak of
but feel so fully when we
won't be able to experience it in person
maybe
ever again
unless we're
very lucky.

And the pink-green-white caladiums
and white begonia on the porch,
and the dress I made for you
and the cuttings of variegated vinca
and autumn clematis....

Older Sister

My sister Helen ate herself to death, some say.
In her mashed potato well she'd pour
the gravy and then lots of peas and mix them
all around. Plenty of country fried steak,
deviled eggs and two pieces of pie
since she couldn't decide between
berry or peach. She reached 250 pounds
after her third child was born and never
went down from there. At 350, diabetes
was diagnosed and arthritis in the knees
so bad she couldn't walk anymore. Then a heart
attack and kidney failure. She survived both.

At sixty-seven they had to put her in a
nursing home. Took very good care of her,
doling out only 1500 calories per day,
searching entering guests for chocolates,
cookies, cakes. In eight months she had lost
a hundred pounds. None of us could hardly
remember her so thin as that.

She died then.

My Fourth Dean

Only grandchild
and a dear manchild
named for his great grandfather
who he never saw and
who I am more like
than most ever realize.

You are the fourth Dean in my
life, Anthony Dean,
great grandson of John Dean,
great nephew of James Dean,
nephew of Timothy Dean.
Your mother was so smart
to put you in that grand procession.

You are this old lady's sweet delight!
So beautiful
so smart, so sensitive,
so knowing and understanding, so
eleven years oldish. You have a
face so expressible and I hope
you never dumb up with blaséness
(if that wasn't a word it is now).

I will not know you as a young man
which doesn't make me too sad.
So you'll be forever
my wonderful little boy.
But wherever you are in the
unknown years ahead,
just rub that 1947 high school
graduation ring I gave you and
look outdoors to the heavens
and I'll be right there,
all the time,
any time.

Donna Lisle Burton

Poem for the Man Who Videoed the Fire

The video shows that at 3:28 a.m.
on July 29, 1991, the house is burning
out of control—rafters blazing, fire
coming out of the roof,
both floors engulfed in smoke, flames.
The owners got out;
only everything they had gathered,
saved in three children
and forty years of marriage
gone.

He was a strange one, the house
owner said of his neighbor.
Mental—but harmless.
Kind of a nuisance.
We didn't know he videoed the fire.

Next scenes show the new house
being built on the ashes of the
old. Sons, daughter, brother
neighbors, townspeople
all came to help paint, hammer,
plumb and watch.

Last scenes are of the
owner and his wife (now dead)
talking in their new home, showing
it off. *He kept trying to get us to*
talk and we neither one wanted to.
Pesty. Mental.
Shot himself in the head not long
afterward.

All those people helping on the house.
Your children ten years ago.
Your deceased wife's voice,
never to be heard again...

That mental pest knew something about
caring.

Doing Less: Settling for More

I truly enjoy doing nothing, at last.
A whole day can now be devoted to
once around the yard—slowly,
a crossword puzzle,
dinner of leftovers,
one good TV show in the evening
(hard to find these days),
and to bed by 10.

I know death is there now.
I acknowledge her and don't act
as if it only happened to
other people.

I worked so hard on a sketch
the other day that I wondered
why I did.
Does it really matter?

That my husband has a pleasant evening matters,
and that my grandson laughs often,
I get plenty of sleep,
I go see my neighbor's twin grand babies;

And

that I wave to the postman,
I see the rime on the mountains,
I not miss the blooming of the
first white crocus:
These are the things that
really matter.

This Heart

If you've been anything,
you've been faithful.
Always there, better than a best friend;
totally dependable.
Your background is not so great
but while inheritance is important,
it's not everything.
I've tried to take care of you too.
Although I like my butter, salt and pasta,
I've tried—at least in recent years—
to assuage my perhaps not so sterling eating habits
with fairly devoted exercise programs.

I, unknowingly, betrayed you with the stint
of liquid diet and you rebelled—the only
way you could (with me in charge) with atrial fibrillation.
Okay, well—sixteen years of warfarin, which
finally led to bleeding problems, changed that regime,
and now it's just you and me, heart; just us.

And you're speaking up now,
demanding some attention—
which you'll get come Monday next.
But I want you to know right now
that whatever you tell the cardiologist,
it will be just fine with me.
You couldn't have served me better
for almost eighty-one years—and I'm ready, my dear friend,
for what's next.

Patty Brought Me Love and Spring This Morning

She said I'm bringing a dinner over for you.
And she did. A meat loaf, large jar
of fresh cut up fruit, wonderful
many grained bread
and some perfect candies.

But she also brought me ten
three-foot pussy willow stalks full of
burgeoning pink buds telling me
I thought of them for you,
you used to have them in your yard.

Her smile was Spring
Her goodbye hug was Spring
She came with her hands and
heart full of spring
and it is yet January.

Is that not love?

Addendum

Only Grandchild

I really am that same old lady
to whose side you used to fly
when I came to visit you.
You never welcomed me
but just fast sat on the couch
as close to me as you could
and shared this thought
that book
your new toy.

How I miss that.

Now, at seventeen, I've become to you
persona non grata and
the closest you ever come near me
is at the dinner table—
where you used to pull the stool up
so you could sit closer to me—
where you now always leave first
the minute you're done eating.
Or eat alone at the computer.

I fear at 85+ I won't live long enough
for you to grow out of this stage.
And so I keep the pictures on my wall
of those days when
you used to think this grandma
was pretty okay to sit as close
as you could to her,
at your home or
hers, all the time.

I still miss that.

Only Daughter

I'm always hoping
(once again, forfeiting NOW)
that I might be around
just a little longer
when foresight may hit late upon you
open your eyes up wide for you and
say *yes, she really did do*
the best she could.

I gave my mother that gift
eons ago, almost before I even
meant it, but knew I would
one day. And she needed that.

But here I am, one foot on the
slippery slope and still
it is not in your mind
that we both need it:
forgiving, each for what
the other could not do then.
Soon there will be not more time
and it will be harder for
both of us—or just you—then.

I hope you see it before
you want to hear
your child say
you did the best you could.

I imagine, he'll need to—
just like every other child on earth.

My Hair

Beautiful, dark brown, shiny,
silver, almost black, head of hair
on the woman in front of me.

Me at six, eight, ten with
a thick head of perfectly straight
dark brown hair—
but I bet I had some red in it,
even then, and how I
hated it.

Shirley Temple curls were what
I longed for; I'd've even kept **brown**
if only I could have had those curls.

Strange enough, by twelve, fourteen, sixteen
I had those curls—no, waves—
and no more rag curlers either;
just waves on me,
a head of hair anyone would be
proud of.

A gift, another grace.

Donna Lisle Burton

A Stolen Day

I grabbed this day and made it mine.
Clouds, blue sky, sunshine,
warm breezes playing with all the leaves.
Birds singing and if you stare long enough
I swear you can actually watch a
peony bud open.

I did what I needed to do.
Cleaned up the kitchen, planned tonight's menu
half hour of enabling exercises
(even beginning to feel the good of them)
clothes off the inside drying line.

And the rest was mine.
Side yard where the wind blows the best,
even a walk around the front yard
(with a walker but feeling stronger)
and a close-up of the front beds—purple
irises out, columbine felt like propagating
everywhere this year, even a hosta
out in full colors and some pink spreading
geranium which I hope will spread
and cover the bare spots.
And the blue bells which have got to be
at least fifty years old as they were at the old
place when I got there thirty years ago and
brought up here fifteen years ago.

And then I sat and read some
Buddhist work which said
get out of your head/come to your senses
and connect with all that is and
just BE.

And Be is what I did and was
for the next hour with all the
above named beauties, breathing
deeply deeply deeply
so much so
had I not been sitting so
tightly in my chair I would have
shinnyed right
on up the oak tree bark and
perched with the cardinal
couple there and would have
joined them in song
had they let me.

A Birthday Gift for Jill

Pretty little lady
with the lovely rings and shoes
always has her arms
so full of gifts
I know one day she will
topple forward with them.

I did not know her
nor she me, but

She was sent as a gift to me,
a real answer to an unreal prayer,
to my diminished world
where I was nursing myself,
cliff-hanging as it were
barely making it.

But I don't know if she really knows
her greatest gift to me.

When you dare to speak your heart
—always a chance-taking trip—
you hope it will be received,
maybe not quite understood or agreed
with or adopted as one's own but
just perceived, validated: seen.

So this lady who
knows herself very well
began to see me and thus
help me see me,
give myself back to me.

You can't give away what you
don't know you have.

Maybe soon,
I'll be engulfed with a plethora of gifts

—of a different kind—

I must give away, so I, too,
will not topple forward with them.

Eternally, Stephen P. Jones

You crawled into my heart
when you confessed that you
kept my book of poems
at your bedside at night.
That keeps on touching me
over and over.
You can't thank someone for
saying that, giving you a
present each time you think of it.

But I can do this:
your beautiful bio with the
perfect picture of you
is at my writing table
and every day,
every time I sit down, hoping to
blossom,
you are there, smiling at me
as if to say
go for it gal!

Stephen P. Jones,
no longer here
but still at it:
my one-man cheering team.

Lost/Found Love

On my wall
so close I can touch it
are four pictures of a man
who is now dead and
who had my heart
for fifty years.

He rescued me when
I was alone, *enciente*, and
in a foreign land called
Dixie.
He found me and fell in
love with me immediately
and forever although I
did not know that then.

When he had to return to his
foreign land Taiwan home,
I could not follow him there then
with my blue eyed blonde
baby girl.
He understood.
Letters flew east and west
for a long time.
Once he sent a gold wedding ring
Keep it he said *and*
soon you will come.

Months became years
and a new man knocked
on my door and
married me, gave my
daughter a name.

Soon this old love sent pictures
of his new bride,
children
and before long
his California home.

And always at Christmas
he called
and always in his voice
in his ordinary words
he said he loved me
when he said *I still miss all of you.*

Once when I went to Hawaii
I stopped in L.A.
to visit my brother and we
all met with him, his family.
You are still beautiful
he whispered
putting an envelope in my hand.
Ten one hundred dollar bills.
Me, unmarried widow
He still married.
You give what you can
when love has to be given.

Later, emails and yet gifts:
a Chinese opera aria,
admonitions about taking care
of myself,
pictures of flowers
lily ponds,
Chinese musical instruments
I do not know.

Then this year
no Christmas call
no card saying *I still
miss all of you so much.*
I send a note
and his *I'm very sick*
answer came soon:
This cannot be cured.

Then followed this note:
*In 1964 I left you.
After fifty years I will
leave again.*

And now I somehow feel free
to put up these pictures
on my wall where I can
see, touch them.
The young Chinese man
holding my new daughter;
two young lovers facing
each other, arm around my back.
The other, holding my hand;
the Chinese-American business man
middle aged;
the white haired retired jet pilot major
standing in front of a plane
he once knew—

somehow now
all mine at last.

About the Author

Donna Lisle Burton grew up in eastern Ohio, beside the Ohio River, in an area of coal mines and steel mills, now mostly gone. Burton has lived in the South for most of her life, working as a special education teacher for four decades in Montgomery and Tuskegee, Alabama, and thereafter in Greenville, SC.

Her poems have been published in *Atlanta Review, Kalliope, Illuminations, The Licking River Review, Main Street Rag, Potpourri,* and other literary magazines. An accomplished painter, portraitist, and photographer, she lives with her husband, Alan, her daughter Cassia, and grandson Dean, near the Blue Ridge Parkway on a dead-end road in Fairview, NC.

Also available from Pisgah Press

Mombie: The Zombie Mom — Barry Burgess
$16.95

Letting Go: Collected Poems 1983-2003 — Donna Lisle Burton
$14.95

Musical Morphine: Transforming Pain One Note at a Time — Robin Russell Gaiser
$17.95

MacTiernan's Bottle — Michael Hopping
$14.95

rhythms on a flaming drum
$16.95

I Like It Here! Adventures in the Wild & Wonderful World of Theatre — C. Robert Jones
$30.00

LANKY TALES
Lanky Tales, Vol. I: The Bird Man & other stories
$9.00
Lanky Tales, Vol. II: Billy Red Wing & other stories
$9.00
Lanky Tales, Vol. III: A Good and Faithful Friend & other stories
$9.00

Red-state, White-guy Blues — Jeff Douglas Messer
$15.95

A Green One for Woody — Patrick O'Sullivan
$15.95

Reed's Homophones: a comprehensive book of sound-alike words — A.D. Reed
$17.95

Swords in their Hands: George Washington and the Newburgh Conspiracy
$24.95 — Dave Richards
Finalist in the USA Book Awards for History, 2014

Trang Sen: A Novel of Vietnam — Sarah-Ann Smith
$19.50

Invasive Procedures: Earthqukes, Calamities, & poems from the midst of life — Nan Socolow
$17.95

THE RICK RYDER MYSTERY SERIES — RF Wilson
Deadly Dancing
$15.95
Killer Weed
$14.95

To order:

Pisgah Press, LLC
PO Box 1427, Candler, NC 28715
www.pisgahpress.com

www.ingramcontent.com/pod-product-compliance
Lightning Source LLC
Chambersburg PA
CBHW071524080526
44588CB00011B/1552